By Edward P. Hamilton

A HISTORY OF MILTON, MASSACHUSETTS

THE FRENCH AND INDIAN WARS

ADVENTURE IN THE WILDERNESS
*The American Journals of
Louis Antoine de Bougainville
1756-1760*

FORT TICONDEROGA
Key to a Continent

Fort Ticonderoga

KEY TO A CONTINENT

Fort Ticonderoga

KEY TO A CONTINENT

by Edward P. Hamilton

with photos

LITTLE, BROWN AND COMPANY · BOSTON · TORONTO

Portions of Chapter 5 and all of Chapter 6 previously appeared in the
author's *The French and Indian Wars,* published by Doubleday and
Company, Inc., copyright 1962 by the Massachusetts Historical Society.

Published simultaneously in Canada
by Little, Brown & Company (Canada) Limited

PRINTED IN THE UNITED STATES OF AMERICA

In Memory of Stephen Pell

Contents

ıııııııııııııııııııııııııııııııııı

(Illustrations appear between pages 116-117)

Fort Ticonderoga

KEY TO A CONTINENT

Prologue

IT WAS ONLY a puny little fortress far out in the wilderness of North America, yet six times within less than a generation great armies marched to assail it.

No fort anywhere in the world has a history such as that possessed by Fort Ticonderoga, yet its active life was but a score of years. Indians, incited, equipped and often led by Frenchmen, slipped silently southward from its gray stone walls to raid the unguarded settlements of New England and the York colony. Sometimes they brought back an unfortunate Englishman or two, whom they knocked on the head and boiled in their brass kettles on the flats below the forts. Occasionally an expedition of Frenchmen stopped there before moving on south against the British. Here it was that Montcalm's army of French regulars, Canadians and Indians assembled in 1757 for the march against Fort William Henry and the siege that led to massacre. Scarce had another year fled before Abercromby, sitting in his tent far from the battlefront, repeatedly flung his great army against the high log wall built by Montcalm's little host. Hour after hour the battle was joined until nightfall at last brought surcease and saw some sixteen hundred British dead and wounded.

Another year rolled by, and Amherst at last seized the fortress, held this year by only a petty garrison of Frenchmen. Long years of peace were to follow, years during which the great stone walls fell into decay, until in the spring of 1775 Ethan Allen thunders demand for surrender in the name of the Great Jehovah. Once more a year passes, and the pitiful, smallpox-ridden American army recoils from its vain attempt at the conquest of Canada, and pauses at Ticonderoga to catch its breath, heal its sick and to hold the frontier against British invasion. It succeeds, but in the following summer, that of 1777, Burgoyne takes the place, shamefully evacuated without fight by its defenders, and marches on to meet his fate at Saratoga. But before the invaders are finally checked at Bemis Heights, gallant John Brown leads an attack on the garrison left at Ticonderoga by the advancing British, succeeds in part, but fails to capture the old stone fortress. Six times armies had marched against the little fort in the course of twenty years; thrice it held, and thrice it fell. No other fort in history can boast of such a record. Such was Ticonderoga, the key to the vital Champlain Valley.

They Followed the Waterways

THROUGH THE narrows at Ticonderoga pressed the great highway of colonial North America, the only practical route between New France and the British colonies, the path that must be followed by all who traveled between the two regions, be they fur traders, stealthy smugglers or great armies. Quite rightly has Ticonderoga been called "The Key to a Continent." He who held the narrows determined who might pass and when.

Today we take roads, highways and great turnpikes for granted, and we have no appreciation of the difficulties of travel in colonial times. In the middle 1700's there were almost no roads in North America, save along the seacoast. A trip over the shore road from Boston to New York normally required at least a week on horseback, ferrying over several rivers. From Boston a road ran west to Worcester and on to Springfield, crossed the Connecticut on a ferry, and then, more trail than road, struggled up the Berkshires, "over mountains that rise like going upstairs," then down to lower levels and on to Claverack on the Hudson, where it met the New York–Albany post road. Yet a keg of rum or a bale of imported sailcloth could move more cheaply and usually more speedily by water, around Cape Cod, along Long Island Sound, and up the Hudson to Albany, than it could had it gone by wagon or pack horse across the Berkshires.

By about 1750 there was a second road to Albany which passed north of Worcester, crossed the Connecticut near Deerfield, and then, probably more pack trail than road, followed up the valley of the Deerfield River, across rugged Hoosuck Mountain, and then over more gentle terrain passed through Williamstown and on to Albany. Robert Treat Paine, who went west in 1755 by this route to serve as chaplain with one of General William Johnson's regiments, has left us a journal and a quaint road map. He recorded that the road west of Williamstown was smooth and level.

The New York–Albany road must have had its attractions and been well served by its inns, for in 1759 General Amherst walked all of its one hundred and sixty miles on foot on his return to New York after the conclusion of the year's campaign. There was a second road to Albany on the west side of the Hudson. The Boston–New York shore road extended to the north at least as far as Portsmouth and south to Annapolis.

Roads west into the foothills of the Appalachians were few in 1750. One ran from Philadelphia to Harrisburg on the Susquehanna, and then, probably only a narrow trail, swung southward through Chambersburg to cross the Potomac near today's Hagerstown, Maryland, and then, now again a wagon road, led down the great Valley of Virginia, the Shenandoah, at least as far as Staunton. Nearly a century later it would be the Valley Pike of Stonewall Jackson's day. Near where the Chambersburg trail crossed the Potomac, it was joined by a road from Alexandria through Frederick, which continued on up the Potomac Valley toward the mountains to Fort Cumberland, the most advanced British post in all this region. Braddock's men would march westward over this miserable road, taking just under a month to cover about 125 miles. South of this Frederick road another ran direct from Alexandria to Winchester in the Valley.

From Chambersburg the pack trail of the fur traders extended west to the Forks of the Ohio, where Pittsburgh stands today. A few years later General Forbes would make it into a wagon road, when he advanced slowly but surely to the capture of Fort Duquesne. From Fort Cumberland another such trail headed toward the Ohio, and it outlined the route Braddock's road soon would follow. But these in 1750 were only trails, narrow and fit only for man or horse; much widening, blasting and corduroying would be needed before they were fit for heavy wagons.

One must not think a colonial road to have been anything like those of today, when almost all have been given a bituminous or concrete top. Look for the crudest, roughest country road that you can find, and you will have an idea of about what they were like — muddy or dusty, rutted and at times almost impassable in places. The day of the stagecoach was still half a century in the future.

Man went by water in colonial North America. The rivers of the country were the highways for both trade and war. Coastal commerce was carried by thousands of little vessels, and the few coastal roads could not compete with waterborne carriers of provisions and merchandise. Tidal rivers and deep estuaries in many places allowed the coastal trade to proceed well inland. The Connecticut was navigable to Hartford, the Hudson to Albany, Chesapeake Bay to Havre de Grace and Head of Elk, the Potomac to Alexandria, and the James to the falls where Richmond was settled in the late 1730's. Further advance westward beyond these points required other forms of transport, travel by foot, by horse and pack train or by small river craft, dugout, barge, canoe or bateau.

A host of little sailing craft plied all along the coastline from Georgia to Nova Scotia, while scows, barges and gondolas were rowed, poled or sailed up and across the bays and estuaries. Goods moved between seacoast towns by water, not by land. And moreover they moved faster that way. The week-long (and often longer) trip by road and ferry from Boston to New York could usually be accomplished in not much over half of that time by going overland to Providence and then by water for the rest of the journey.

Any real penetration of the interior had, practically speaking, to be made by water. The great Appalachian mountain chain determined that. Extending from almost the banks of the St. Lawrence all the way south to the new colony of Georgia, these mountains presented a great barrier to any land movement westward. True, you could penetrate them on foot, but at most you could carry only perhaps seventy-five pounds—which must include food and your personal equipment before you could add traps, trade goods or merchandise. Or you could take a string of pack horses, each carrying a load of some two hundred pounds; but this must include at least some forage, for grass was always scanty in the great forests. A boat, on the other hand, would take any load you wanted, provided the craft did not become too large to handle on the inland waters, and it could be paddled, rowed or poled with much less effort than was required to force one's way through the primeval forests and over the rugged mountains.

Water transport, of course, had its drawbacks — waterways did not always go where one wished, and often they were interrupted by falls and rapids, or became too small or shallow. Recourse then was made to overland carry of boat and cargo — portaging, it was called — until another waterway was reached. Certain portages were of great strategic value and in many cases forts were built to control them. Examples are Fort Niagara, which covered the vital passage to the Far West; Fort Edward, where commenced the two portages to Lake George and Lake Champlain; and

Fort Stanwix on the Mohawk waterway. At important and often used portages improvements sometimes were made to facilitate passage. Road work of course was important, and at Niagara the French at one time kept ox teams permanently stationed, while at the short but busy carry by the falls of the Oswego River some genius devised a series of rollers so that bateaux could be rolled across without necessity of unloading them.

Fortunately the rivers of North America so interlaced their tributaries that portaging was usually necessary only for a few miles at most, a minor inconvenience in view of the relative ease of the rest of the journey. By far the longest water route of North America was that up the St. Lawrence over a number of short portages to Lake Ontario, then a fairly arduous carry by Niagara, followed by travel on the open lakes all the way to the site of the future Chicago, where at times of high water a bateau could often be floated over the divide into the headwaters of the Illinois River, then on to the Mississippi and New Orleans.

The other great disadvantage of water transport was that for at least three months the rivers and lakes in northern parts were frozen solid. But this was not too serious, for military campaigns were usually undertaken in summer. In winter a man could haul his furs or trade goods behind him on a sled over the frozen water surface almost as easily as he could have paddled or poled. Here the British had a real advantage over the French, for their waterways were open longer. Spring came late in New France.

Unfortunately for the British colonists, practically all of their rivers led only into the mountains and furnished no thoroughfare to the west, but there were two most important exceptions; the Mohawk corridor, and that of the Hudson-Champlain Valley. The Mohawk River, interrupted by two or three waterfalls which required only short carries, ran from the Hudson due west to today's Rome, New York, in those days called "The Great Carrying Place." A relatively short land carry then led overland to the waters of a tortuous and swampy creek which, by twisting through humid, mosquito-ridden woods, at last entered Lake Oneida, whence the Oswego River flowed, with but a single waterfall, into Lake Ontario. This was Britain's only water route to the west, and it was of vast importance. Indians had long brought furs eastward along the Mohawk to Albany, and by 1721 the fur trading post of Oswego on Lake Ontario had been established. This post at once became a thorn in the flank of New France, for not only did it represent a British penetration into lands claimed by the French King, but it also very largely diverted furs from the French West to the Dutch merchants of Albany. Moreover, this westward corridor gave the British direct access to the waters of the Far West and an opportunity through intelligent use of naval power to control all that vast land. Today it is hard to understand why Britain, thoroughly imbued with the vital importance of her navy on salt water, failed to extend similar thinking to the great inland lakes of North America. Had she done so, the last French and Indian war would have been concluded much sooner and with greater ease.

Farther to the south conditions were quite different, for all the rivers had their headwaters in the lofty Appalachians and their river valleys faded out into the mountain slopes. Water transport speedily came to an end, and only man's two feet or the pack horse could penetrate the great mountain ranges, which, forming a massive barrier all the way from the Mohawk to the plains of Georgia, cut off the seaboard colonies from the great West.

Geography was kinder to the French, for nature had given them waterways which offered easy access to the Great Lakes, the waters of the Ohio and even the Mississippi itself. Thus the French could establish posts beyond the mountain barrier and attempt to hold the heartland against an advance of British settlers. This they were able to do with considerable success, largely through the use of raiding Indians who were based on French forts in the Ohio country. These posts, although relatively easy of access by water from Montreal, were nevertheless at a great distance from their base of supply, and it was not expedient to attempt formal military action eastward through the mountains, here just as much a barrier to the French as to the English. Offensive Indian raids backed by forts capable of defensive action were sufficient to hold the colonists in check south of the Mohawk. Major military expeditions by the British would be another matter, but such expeditions were still in the future in 1754. To the north two opposing civilizations, the tight despotism of New France and the separate little independent democracies that were the British colonies, faced each other at relatively close range in the Hudson-Champlain Valley, where the great north-south waterway of colonial days made passage simple and easy. The British pushed up the Hudson and the French up the Richelieu into Lake Champlain. It was on this great waterway of North America that the two would first meet in battle.

Most of the watercraft used on these inland rivers were a product of the country, new to European eyes. The earliest of all was probably the log dugout, a form of boat common to primeval man, but abandoned by the Indian in later centuries. During the colonial period and later white men on the Hudson made highly refined dugouts, well shaped and thinned down to fairly light weight. In the mid-1700's, at least, these dugouts were usually propelled by a man standing and paddling with a short oar. Dugouts were quite narrow and must have required a nice sense of balance. The really important boats of fresh-water North America throughout many years were the canoe of the Indian, the bateau of the white man and, to a lesser extent, the whaleboat.

The northern Indian made his canoe of birch. It was surprisingly like our modern version except that birchbark instead of painted canvas formed the waterproof envelope. The bark, however, did not furnish the structural strength, for under this outer envelope long thin wooden strips gave lengthwise strength just as they do in our modern canvas canoes, and there also were many light ribs. Had an Indian canoe of two hundred years ago been covered with canvas instead of birchbark it would have been little different from its modern counterpart. One perhaps wonders how an Indian, working only with tools of stone and bone, could have fashioned these long slender strips of thin wood. If the proper kind of wood is thoroughly soaked and then sufficiently pounded with a smooth stone it can be peeled off in thin layers, each growth ring in sequence. These then will split easily along their length, giving the wooden strips necessary both for canoe-building and basket-making. When dried out again the wood regains most of its strength. A birchbark canoe was an excellent and long-lived watercraft and needed only occasional patching of the bark as holes or cracks made their appearance. These canoes varied in size from those intended to carry two men and their baggage up to the master canoes of the Great Lakes region, thirty-five feet long or more and carrying a crew of eight or ten in addition to some three tons of trade goods, provisions or furs.

Farther to the south, not far south of Ticonderoga, there were fewer and fewer birch trees suitable for canoes, and the Mohawks were forced to make theirs of elm bark, a much less suitable material. When wet it becomes soft and flabby, when dry it shrinks badly and often develops splits. The elm canoes were usually made each year and then discarded, although sometimes attempts were apparently made to preserve them by burying them in damp sand. All in all they were considered to be a most inferior form of boat. They differed basically from the birch canoe in that the heavy thick bark alone was depended on for lengthwise strength, and only a few ribs were used.

The white man's workhorse was the bateau, a double-ended, flat-bottomed, lapstreaked boat of shallow draft. It was much like the modern Gloucester dory except for the small stern transom characteristic of the latter. The bateau was the common watercraft of inland North America, and it was built in thousands, yet no complete specimen is known to exist today. The bottom plankings of a number have been found in Lake George in recent years, but most of their ribs and side plankings have rotted away. There is, however, still hope that a complete specimen may yet be found, or at least reassembled from separate parts. The Maritime Museum at Greenwich, England, has a contemporary drawing giving lines and dimensions of two colonial bateaux, while the Swedish naturalist Peter Kalm, a great traveler, has left us a clear description of bateaux that he had seen in 1749. Those in use around Albany were usually from eighteen to twenty-four feet long with a greatest width of about three and a half feet. The sides, particularly amidships, were nearly vertical, making it easier to pole the craft in shallow water. Such a shape made a poor boat indeed for the rough water of an open lake, and bateaux for such employment had more flaring sides than those intended for river work. Kalm, an observant man with an inquiring mind, wrote that he had seen nothing like these bateaux anywhere in Europe. The design may have developed in America to suit the local needs, or it may well be that the resulting form is the simplest and quickest one suitable for shallow water that can be nailed together. The type appears in America in clearly defined form at least by the early 1700's, and, save for the considerably modified lumberman's bateau of later years, it completely disappears in the early 1800's. Oddly enough, the Roman pleasure galleys recovered from Lake Nemi shortly before World War II, and later burned by the Germans, had tenders which from photographs appear to be practically identical in form with the bateaux of our colonial days.

These boats varied in size from the smaller ones in use around Albany to great craft up to forty-five feet long, capable of carrying as much as twelve tons. These larger examples, usually rigged with sail, were for use on the Great Lakes or the Mississippi and were too large for many of the smaller rivers. French bateaux normally were considerably larger than those of the British, a fact which worked much to the former's advantage in the last French war when bateaux of the two nations met on Lake Ontario. It was then found that the British could not stand up to fire their muskets for fear of capsizing their craft, while their enemies could. British bateaux used on the Mohawk averaged about twenty-five feet long overall. Lewis Evans, mapmaker and geographer, wrote that the usual Mohawk bateau was manned by two men and would carry freight of about three-quarters of a ton, just about what was considered a wagonload. The examples that carried Abercromby's army over Lake George to its 1758 attack on Fort Carillon at Ticonderoga each carried twenty-two soldiers and their provisions for a month. These typically consisted of two barrels of salt pork, four of hard bread or flour, and a few sacks of dried peas, rice or cornmeal, giving a total load, both men and provisions, of about three tons.

Charles Carroll of Carrollton, who went north to Canada in 1776 as a commissioner of the Continental Congress, kept an interesting journal. It tells us that the bateaux then being used to move troops down Lake George were thirty-six feet long by eight wide and could hold thirty to forty men. They had a mast to which a small squaresail or a blanket could be fixed, but this was useless unless the wind came from almost directly astern. Some of these boats even had awnings. Carroll was interested to see that General Schuyler had devised a machine at the foot of Lake George which picked each bateau out of the water and loaded it on a special four-wheeled carriage for transport over the portage down to Lake Champlain.

Bateaux could be hurriedly and roughly built. Sometimes, as in examples found in Lake George, part of the bark was left on the ribs, so crudely were they finished. The planks for the sides and bottom, of course, had to be sawed out from logs, either with two men and a sawpit, or, if one were in luck, by a little water-powered sawmill. It is on record that six men could put an average bateau together in two days, including sawing the planks. This is only a little longer than Peter Kalm found necessary to build an elm-bark canoe.

The gondola appeared on Lake Champlain in the Revolution, but the name, if not the precise form, is found as early as the closing years of the seventeenth century in New Hampshire. Those built on Lake Champlain in 1776 were flat-bottomed craft of about forty-five feet in length, carrying a fairly heavy cannon in their rounded bows and a smaller piece amidships on either side. They had a single mast with square mainsail and topsail. The stern was pointed with a little rake and carried a rudder, and the craft was built with quite heavy timbers. Gondolas were intended to be rowed quite as much as sailed. They were poor sailers except before the wind, but could stand surprisingly rough water. I had often wondered about their ancestry and searched for an indication without success until I realized that the gondola was merely a great bateau, its bow rounded and enlarged to support the weight of its forward gun, and its timbers strengthened throughout to carry the weight of its cannon.

On the larger rivers and lakes barges were sometimes used. They were merely great scows. Lewis Evans wrote that those on the Delaware River were made like troughs, forty or fifty feet long, six or seven wide and perhaps three deep, their ends sloped on the underside to decrease water resistance. They drew little over a foot and a half when loaded. On the lakes both nations launched little sailing vessels during the Seven Years War — some for cargo-carrying, others armed for battle, and none probably much over fifty feet long; but during the Revolution both the Americans and the British had rather sizable warships on Lake Champlain. In 1756 the British were well on their way to possessing quite an imposing little navy on Lake Ontario, but they dawdled too long and Montcalm's spirited raid on Oswego caught most of the vessels either on the stocks or still without armament. During the colonial period neither side appeared to appreciate the decisive effect that a naval supremacy on the Great Lakes would have on the contest for Canada. The French after the fall of Oswego had acquired, through construction as well as capture, an important little fleet, yet they failed to utilize it. Bradstreet's dash against Fort Frontenac was made only in bateaux, and it caught the French fleet tied up in harbor, crews understrength on some vessels, while others were both unmanned and unrigged. There were of course serious problems in maintaining a fleet on western waters, particularly that of safeguarding the vessels when winter had locked them fast in the thick ice, easy prey for the torch of a raiding party. One certain but somewhat drastic solution was to unrig and empty the hull and then sink it safely below the surface until spring allowed the process to be reversed. These problems, difficult as they may have seemed, could have been resolved, and had the effort and money of Braddock's vain attempt on Fort Duquesne been devoted to putting the British Navy on Lake

Ontario, the war would have been materially shortened.

Finally, the whaleboat deserves a brief mention. They were used for scouting on Lakes George and Champlain by Robert Rogers and his Rangers. These boats were collected on Cape Cod, Martha's Vineyard and Nantucket and taken up the Hudson to Albany and then over the portage to the lakes. We do not know just what they were like, but it seems probable that they were little different from the later New Bedford whaleboat except that they would have no center-board, and probably no sail. Their light weight and the ease with which they could be rowed made them ideal for scouting expeditions. In the course of one raid Rogers carried his whaleboats from Lake George to Lake Champlain about six miles overland and across a mountain chain as well.

Mention was made earlier of the Hudson-Champlain waterway, the great thoroughfare along which nations, first Indians, then French and British, and finally British and Americans, were to meet in battle for centuries. From a point some two score miles north of Albany the Hudson River runs, straight almost as a tightened string, due south to the city of New York. The little oceangoing vessels of colonial days could ply their way north to Albany, and there discharge their cargoes, which then would be carried either by wagon over the sandy plains to Schenectady and on up the Mohawk by water, or, if intended for the north, a combination of water transport and land carriage by the little falls and rifts of the upper Hudson would bring the goods to Fort Edward, built in 1755 on the site of Lydius's trading post of earlier times. Here there was a choice of overland routes before the Champlain waterway could be attained. One could proceed over the almost water-level carry to Fort Anne, or, as an alternative, climb the steep carry up to the head of Lake George. Both were about the same length, some dozen miles or so, but once Fort Anne was reached there remained another similar distance along the twisting, muddy Wood Creek, where muskrat houses were seen by the hundreds, and there were great marshes where the wild duck lay in vast flocks. The Lake George carry gave access to some thirty-five miles of travel over the waters of one of the most beautiful lakes of North America, and then, down-hill over a mile-long carry, one reembarked his bateau or canoe into Lake Champlain, some twenty miles north of the mouth of Wood Creek. There remained a hundred miles of travel before the northern end of Champlain was reached, and one entered the Richelieu River, tributary to the mighty St. Lawrence. There were two or three short rapids in the Richelieu, some or all of which could be run if the water was not too low. At worst they were but minor portages.

And so the Hudson-Champlain Valley with only minor annoyances allowed free travel from New York all the way north to Montreal. This was the route of the smugglers and of trade, and when war came, it was only by water transport over this great thoroughfare that the tools and supplies of combat could be carried. The Hudson-Champlain waterway connected two very different civilizations, doomed to mutual attempts at conquest, and it is obvious that military effort would necessarily be canalized along this great artery of North America.

The place where the Lake George carry enters the narrow southern arm of Lake Champlain was called Ticonderoga by the Indians, and, controlling as it did both routes between the lake and the Hudson, it was the critical point on the entire waterway which extended from the Atlantic to the St. Lawrence. From Champlain's 1609 fight until Burgoyne was at last overcome at Saratoga in 1777 men were to fight for this critical point on the narrows of Lake Champlain. He who held Ticonderoga did indeed hold the "key to a continent" in his hands.